A. J. Foyt celebrates his fourth Indy victory in the winner's circle.

The Indy 500

Jim Murphy

Illustrated with photographs

CLARION BOOKS

TICKNOR & FIELDS: A HOUGHTON MIFFLIN COMPANY

New York

For Carol and Tom Walsh—very special friends
who always travel in the fast lane

CLARION BOOKS
Ticknor & Fields, a Houghton Mifflin Company

Copyright © 1983 by Jim Murphy

PRINTED IN THE U.S.A.

Library of Congress Cataloging in Publication Data
Murphy, Jim, 1947–
    The Indy 500.

    Includes index.
    Summary: Takes the reader through an Indy 500, including the crash of
one of the cars. Discusses the car, track, pit crew, etc.
    1. Indianapolis Speedway Race—Juvenile literature.
[1. Indianapolis Speedway Race.   2. Automobile racing]
I. Title. II. Title: Indy Five Hundred.
GV1033.5.155M87   1983   796.7′2′06877252   83-2093
ISBN 0-89919-151-7

Book design by Maria Epes

V 10 9 8 7 6 5 4 3 2

Acknowledgments

The author wishes to thank the following individuals and corporations for their generous help and encouragement: Al Bloemker, Vice-President, Indianapolis Motor Speedway; Ron McQueeney, Director of Photography, Indianapolis Motor Speedway; Dan Luginbuhl, Vice-President—Communications, Penske Corporation; Jim Cutler, photographer, Penske Racing Team; Jack Brannan, Director—External Relations, Norton Company; Martin A. Kish, Marketing Communications Coordinator, Valvoline Oil Company; Harvey Duck, Publicity Director, STP Corporation; Dave Hederich, Public Relations Manager—Racing, Goodyear Tire and Rubber Company; Larry Rubin, International Association of Machinists and Aerospace Workers; the United States Auto Club.

Photographs are used through the courtesy of: Indianapolis Motor Speedway, 12, 15, 34, 60, 74; IMS/Duffy, 62; IMS/Dan Francis, 21, 67, 70, 77, 78; IMS/John Gray, 72; IMS/Jim Haines, 23, 51; IMS/Harlen Hunter, 14, 45, 47, 68, 69; IMS/Steve Lingenfelter, 52, 84, 85; IMS/Ron McQueeney, 33; IMS/Mark Reed, 58; IMS/Bob Scott, 49, 50, 61; IMS/Larry Smith, 28, 29; IMS/Steve Snoddy, 82; IMS/Denis Sparks, 8; IMS/Jeff Stephenson, 80; IMS/Rick Wall, 56, 59; IMS/Bill Watson, 22, 79, 87; IMS/Van Wildman, 65, 75; IMS/Debbie Young, 64; Valvoline, 2, 16, 17, 18, 19, 24, 36, 54; Goodyear, 26, 31, 38, 41, 42; Penske Racing, 10, 44, 51; Penske Racing/Jim Cutler, 40; Machinists Union, 48; Norton, 53.

For information about IMS photos write: the Director of Photography, Indianapolis Motor Speedway, 4790 West 16th Street, Box 24152, Speedway, Indiana 46224.

Contents

Car 58 sweeps through a turn.

Introduction

A line of race cars charges down the straightaway at nearly 200 miles per hour. Engines screaming, the cars are blurs of color as they soar through the sharp turn. Some of the drivers are already legends in motor racing—A. J. Foyt, Mario Andretti, the Unser brothers, Johnny Rutherford. Others, such as Kevin Cogan and Josele Garza, are lesser known but just as determined. But the one thing they all have in common is that they're trying to win the biggest and most important auto race in the world.

This book takes a behind-the-scenes look at the Indy 500. It tells how the cars are prepared. It introduces the many people responsible for keeping them repaired and running. And it describes the grueling practice session and qualifying runs that fill the weeks before the race. Finally, it shows what it's really like to be behind the wheel of a powerful racing machine—and why each year during the Memorial Day weekend thirty-three skilled drivers risk their lives to compete in the Indy 500.

Cogan showed no signs of handling problems when he qualified his
Norton Spirit in 1982 at 204.082 mph, the fifth fastest time ever.

1

The Challenge of Indy

Kevin Cogan brings his Norton Spirit through turns one and two and shoots down the ⅝-of-a-mile-long straightaway. Halfway down it, the 675-horsepower Cosworth engine has pushed the car's speed to almost 200 miles per hour (mph).

As he approaches turn three, his car is only a foot from the outside wall. Cogan is aware of the strip of white concrete to his right, but he's concentrating on the upcoming turn. The slightest error could put him out of control and into that wall. At the last possible instant, he twists the steering wheel an inch to the left. His car dives into the turn. But as it does, Cogan feels the front tires slide on the pavement. To keep his car on the track, he actually has to oversteer into the turn.

Once through the quarter-mile turn, he eases off the accelerator and drops low on the track. He'll have to bring his car into the pits for more adjustments.

Scenes like this are repeated hundreds of times during the long practice period. The drivers for the more than eighty cars entered each year test and retest their machines. They're looking for as much speed as possible, of course. The qualifying runs are just days away and only the thirty-three fastest will make it into the actual race. But the drivers also want their cars to handle perfectly. That's because the Indianapolis Motor Speedway is one of the most difficult race tracks in the world.

The Speedway was built in 1909. The original owners designed it as a giant 2½-mile-long rectangle so they could put up grand-

Ray Harroun didn't have much protection as he sped down the brick straightaway. He has no gloves, windshield, or seat belt. And his headgear is made of thin leather. *Below:* This diagram highlights the main features of the Speedway today.

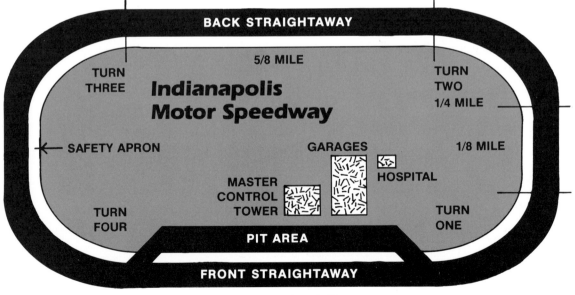

BACK STRAIGHTAWAY

5/8 MILE

TURN THREE

Indianapolis Motor Speedway

TURN TWO

1/4 MILE

← SAFETY APRON

GARAGES

1/8 MILE

MASTER CONTROL TOWER

HOSPITAL

TURN FOUR

TURN ONE

PIT AREA

FRONT STRAIGHTAWAY

START/FINISH LINE

stands on the two long and two short straightaways. The straights were 50 feet wide, while the width in the turns increased to just 60 feet. In addition, the four turns were very sharp and only slightly banked or angled. The steeper the bank at a track the easier it is for a driver to keep his car on the track. The slight banking at Indy means that a speeding car tends to drift up high toward the wall when taking a turn.

Two years after opening, Ray Harroun drove his Marmon Wasp to victory in the first Indy 500. Harroun averaged 74.59 mph during the race.

Since it opened, the Speedway has undergone many changes. The original track of crushed stone and tar disintegrated during the first season. So a firm driving surface of 3,200,000 paving bricks was put in. This is why the Speedway is often referred to as the Brickyard. Fifty years later, right after the 1961 race, the bricks were covered by asphalt. Only a 36-inch commemorative strip of bricks remains at the start/finish line. Other changes included a bigger pit area, a 32-inch high concrete retaining wall with safety fences, and enlarged grandstands.

Despite all these improvements, the basic shape of the track has not changed in seventy-four years. It is still very narrow with extremely sharp turns. Increasing the danger is a thin safety apron of grass to the inside of the asphalt roadway. The safety apron is only about 100 feet wide, ending with a 4-foot-tall steel guard rail to protect the spectators. If a car goes out of control, it will either hit the outside concrete wall or the inside guardrail—or both.

The track is so confining, one driver has compared circling it to "driving down a long, narrow hallway and making a sharp turn into the bedroom."

The shape of the Speedway contrasts dramatically with the design of most modern speedways, which are usually oval-shaped with steep bankings. This means the drivers only have to maneuver through two long, smooth turns each lap. And if a car

It's early morning and the Speedway crew checks turn three for paper, chunks of metal, and oil. An Indy car at speed can go from where the camera is to the trucks in two seconds.

does go out of control, the driver usually has a safety apron of over 300 feet in which to wrestle his car to a safe stop.

But the unique shape of the Speedway establishes the challenge of Indy: How to keep a 200-mph car on a track designed for machines that went only 85 mph.

To meet this challenge, Indy cars have changed a great deal over the past six decades. Gaston Chevrolet (page 15 at top) took the 1920 race in this bullet-shaped car. He averaged 88.62 mph.

Chevrolet's car is built high off the brick surface and has 3-inch-wide spoked wheels. Mechanics often rode with the drivers in those days. If a car broke down on the back straightaway, the mechanic would hop out and repair it. And if he couldn't get it going, he and the driver could always push it to the garages for more work.

Thirty-nine years later, in 1959, Rodger Ward roared to victory at over 135.857 mph. Ward's car is lower to the driving surface

Chevrolet's car has only the number 4 painted on it, while Ward's is loaded with the decals of his sponsors. Ward also has a hard protective helmet, seat belt, windshield, and roll bar.

Gordon Johncock in his 1964 rear-engine car.

and more streamlined. This shape made it easier for it to plow through the air than Chevrolet's car. But it still looked like a long, narrow bullet.

The biggest design change happened in 1961, when the first rear-engine car ran at Indy. Its design was based on the European cars that dominated the Grand Prix racing circuit.

A rear engine meant there was no driveshaft running under the car. The car could be built even lower to the ground than Ward's car. What's more, the driver didn't have to sit straight up while racing and be hit by rushing air. He could sit on the floor of the car with his feet stretched out into the machine's nose. And without an engine, the nose could be more pointed. Fatter tires increased traction through the turns.

These cars had smaller engines so they weren't as fast down the straights as the older front-engine machines. But they took turns so well that they began beating the older cars easily. After a rear-engine machine smashed the Indy qualifying records in 1964, A. J. Foyt began referring to his front-engine car as "an antique." By 1965 all the top drivers had rear-engined cars.

Designers went to work to make these cars lighter and faster. Fiberglas and aluminum replaced the heavier sheet metal for the outer body. Aluminum and other light metals were used in the engine, chassis, and wheels. But the cars were so light that at high speeds they lifted off the track and were hard to control. This brought in the next phase of the rear-engine revolution, when wings were added to the machines in the late 1960s.

At first, the wings were very small and attached to the side of the car just in front of the rear wheel.

Later, wings were added to the car's nose, and a large wing was placed behind the engine.

These wings work the same way they would on an airplane, but with an important difference. They are upside down on the car. As air passes over them, it actually pushes the car down against the road surface for better traction. The wings produce 800 pounds of downward force.

Before long, vents were built into each side of the body. Air

The tiny wings helped Al Unser to dominate the 1970 race. His P. J. Colt won easily, leading for 190 of the 200 laps.

The cowboy hat beside the words *Gilmore Racing Team* is the trade-mark of A. J. "Super Tex" Foyt.

enters the vent openings just behind the front tire. It is channeled over the upper surface of the body. Like the wings, this pushes the car down against the track.

The vents have another purpose. Inside the vent the rushing air hits radiators and helps cool the engine.

The modern Indy car is wedge-shaped, with a sleek, one-piece Fiberglas body that's 15 feet long. The highest part of the machine is the rear wing and it is only 32 inches tall! The shape helps the car knife through the air easily. And these cars are extremely light, weighing anywhere from 1,425 to 1,500 pounds. That's lighter than most two-seater sports cars.

The latest design change can't even be seen. Designers made the bottom underneath the car nearly touch the road surface. This forms a venturi. As air flows through the narrow space it creates a vacuum that actually sucks the car down against the track. This improves road handling and increases lap speeds. Cars with a wing/venturi design are called "ground effects" cars.

An entire year is needed to design and build these complicated

Ground effects help A. J. Foyt's car hug the track during one of his practice laps in 1981.

Andretti and his mechanics discuss the car's handling.

ground effects cars. But even then, the car isn't ready to run at the Speedway. That's why Indy has the longest practice session of any motor race.

For three weeks and a day before the race, the drivers try to get to know their cars. They'll do endless laps to see how they take the turns, how fast they accelerate.

Qualifying runs take place during the second and third weekends of practice. But even if a car qualifies on its first attempt, the driver will take it out several times afterward. He wants to find a little more speed or make his car handle better.

"The idea is to pretend you're the car," Johnny Parsons explains. "I forget I'm a human and begin to think the way a car would if it had its own mind."

When a driver finds a problem, he'll bring the car into the pits to discuss it with the mechanics and designer.

The search for both speed *and* perfect handling is part of the challenge of Indy. The narrow track and wall simply don't allow room to spin out and regain control of the car.

The most common handling problems are "push" and "being loose." A car that pushes slides its front tires along the pavement. It's like an eraser rubbing across a piece of paper. A badly pushing car is said to be "plowing."

When a car is "loose," its rear tires slide more than the front tires. The looser a car is the more likely it is to spin out.

Simple adjustments to correct either of these problems can be done in the pit area. A tire might be replaced. The suspension system can be adjusted. The wings can be tilted to produce more or less downward force. When the work is done, the car goes out and runs a few more laps to see if the adjustments have helped.

More complicated work is done at the team's garage. Forty-four tiny garages face one another across a small driveway—an area known as Gasoline Alley. Day and night, the mechanics tune and retune the engines for maximum power. They inspect brake systems for worn parts. It's not unusual for the mechanics to

One mechanic works in tight quarters under the car, while another examines the right side. The car's front wing sits next to the pit wall at the left.

completely tear apart and rebuild a car several times during the practice session.

In addition to speed and handling, the mechanics want the car to be durable. It's been estimated that the wear a car gets during the 500-mile race is equal to 50,000 miles of ordinary street driving. In fact, Indy has often been referred to as a "breakdown race." No wonder. Only eight cars were still running at the end of the 500 in 1982.

To guard against sudden breakdowns, each of the car's 5,000

Many mechanics put in over 300 hours of work during the three weeks of practice. Here two check a car's wheel alignment.

parts is examined for wear. Many are x-rayed, and if microscopic cracks are found, the parts are replaced. Even with this kind of care, the unexpected can still happen. Bob Frey was going along smoothly when pressure inside his engine caused it to explode. This is called "blowing an engine" and is one of the most common reasons for a breakdown.

For twenty-two days, the drivers and mechanics search for the very best setup for their cars. If a car is operating well, the driver can do over 210 mph on the long straightaways and 185 mph

A smoking engine is a sure sign that it's blown. Frey has his right arm raised in the air. This lets everyone know that he's unhurt and has control of his car.

through the turns. He can do this without ever lifting his foot off the accelerator. And each driver has the same goal: to qualify for one of the thirty-three spots in the Indy 500.

A. J. seems like a big, friendly bear here, but on the track there is no one more competitive.

2

There's Only One Indy

It's 10 o'clock—one hour before the first day of qualifying begins. The garage of car 14 buzzes with activity. Two mechanics are carefully putting together the engine. An assistant is busy taping up the joints and exposed screws of the car's body. The tape allows air to flow over these areas smoothly and reduces vibration. The driver, A. J. Foyt, looks over the work approvingly, then leaves to examine the track.

Foyt is the center of attention as he moves through a crowded Gasoline Alley. He's driven over 8,700 miles at the Brickyard and earned $1,400,000 while doing it—both records. And he's won the race more than anyone else, an amazing four times. If anyone is an expert on the Speedway, it is A. J. Foyt. He leaves the garage area and enters the pits.

Already 100,000 people have gathered to watch the qualifying runs. They want to see if anyone has the speed to beat Teo Fabi's four-lap record of 207.395 mph. More important, they want to see who will win the pole position.

Foyt glances skyward; it's slightly overcast and cool. He's glad about this. Earlier he drew a low qualifying number, so he'll be one of the first on the track. He knows that with the track cooler his engine generates more horsepower. He can run an extra 3 mph faster.

Fans in the pit area bleachers spot Foyt and call to him, wishing him luck. He flashes them a quick smile and waves, but he doesn't really see them. Instead, he's thinking of his qualifying

The front row for the 1981 500. Pole winner Bobby Unser was forty-seven years old then; in the middle is Mike Mosley, age thirty-five; while Foyt, age forty-six, is on the outside.

laps, feeling the car's powerful acceleration down the straights. He knows he has the speed to take the pole for his seventh time. All he has to do is concentrate all of his attention on his driving.

It's hard to think of A. J. Foyt and some of the other drivers as highly conditioned athletes. Many of them are overweight, and a number of them are in their late thirties and forties—long past the age when athletes in other professional sports have retired.

But a driver has to be in extremely good physical condition. If his car doesn't break down on race day, he'll be on the track for almost three and a half hours. During that time he'll make 800 left turns, while the temperature in the car climbs above 100 degrees. A driver can expect to sweat off 10 pounds by the end of the race.

Drivers must also have excellent hand/eye coordination. An Indy car can cover over 300 feet in just one second. A slight miscalculation in heavy traffic can cause an accident.

Stamina and coordination are so important at the Speedway that every driver must pass a difficult rookie driving test. This is usually done at the beginning of the practice session.

The test has two parts. First, the driver must do twenty laps (50 miles) at 160 mph. He isn't allowed to go more than 1 mph below or 2 mph above this speed. Since Indy cars don't have speedometers, the driver must know how to control his speed by the way the car feels. After this, he does another twenty laps at over 165 mph.

Veteran drivers are stationed at each turn. They make sure the rookie takes the turns smoothly and in complete control of his car lap after lap. Indy cars often run within 12 inches of one another, especially while passing. It's essential that every driver handle his car consistently over the long race.

Aside from having these physical qualities, a driver has to be able to concentrate. Once behind the wheel, he must shut out all thoughts of his family or friends or personal problems. Drivers will even continue to race after a teammate has been killed in an accident.

A driver will focus his mind completely on his car and driving. He's alert to the slightest change in the sound of the engine. A tiny vibration tells him a tire might be wearing down. He knows where he is on the track and where other drivers are around him.

A driver must process all of this information quickly. It takes only about eight seconds to go through turns one and two. In the short straight between the turns the car might come within a foot of the wall. There's no time to think of anything but driving here. Then the driver shoots down the ⅝-of-a-mile-long straight, covering the distance in eight to ten seconds. This doesn't give him much time to check his gauges, talk by radio with the pit, and get ready to go into turn three.

But sometimes even the best driver's mind will wander from the race. When a driver's concentration is broken, it's called "brain fade." A second of brain fade can put a car out of control at 160 mph.

Each driver gets three attempts at qualifying. For each one he can take three practice laps. These let him work the car up to

A slight error and Patrick Bedard found himself going backward. Bedard locked up his tires which caused them to smoke.

Then he turned the front wheels to the right, hoping to spin the car away from the wall.

speed gradually and make sure it is running well. If it isn't, he can pull off the track for repairs and make another attempt to qualify later in the day. If everything seems fine with the car, the driver will then do four laps (10 miles) full out.

Photoelectric clocking devices time the speed of the cars to within 1/100 mph. The car with the fastest average speed for the four laps wins the inside position on the first row. This is the pole position. Along with winning the pole, the driver of the fastest car also wins $20,000 and prizes. The other cars are assigned starting positions according to their speed.

One odd rule complicates all this. Cars that qualify on the first weekend always start ahead of cars that qualify on the second. This encourages teams to get their machines set up as early as possible. But it also makes it possible for a slower car to start ahead of a faster one simply because the driver and crew were

A second later, he's got the car almost under control. Notice Bedard had his head turned so he could see where he was headed at all times.

able to get it ready and on the track before time ran out on the first weekend.

In one way, doing qualifying laps is easier than driving in the race. The driver is alone on the track. He doesn't have to worry about traffic. He can concentrate fully on maintaining his speed and staying in the "groove."

The groove is the easiest and fastest route through the turns. Usually it is darker than the rest of the track because rubber from the tires gets ground into it during practice. Getting the car below the groove causes the rear to become loose. Above the groove is an area known as the "marbles." Up there, tiny balls of rubber worn from the tires collect. A car up in the marbles can slide along out of control.

Because only the thirty-three fastest cars will qualify, the drivers go much faster than in the race. When Rick Mears set a four-lap record in 1982 (since broken by Teo Fabi), his straightaway speeds approached 220 mph. But with each lap his car's handling got looser. "In turn three, I got the car sideways a little," Mears said afterward. "We were wondering if I was going to make it."

Drivers will push their cars and themselves to the limit to win a starting position in the front row. These cars begin the race with a full straightaway lead over the slowest cars. It's nearly impossible for the last rows to make up this distance. And because there is little traffic up front, the first few rows tend to leap ahead and away from the rest of the field.

The driver who qualifies with the slowest time is said to be the "man on the bubble." If anyone can go faster than this driver, even by a fraction of a second, the man on the bubble will be bumped from the starting field.

Often the man on the bubble hangs around the start/finish line to watch the other drivers run their qualifying laps. As drivers get closer and closer to bumping him, this driver's expression might seem very sad. Then he's said to be "hanging crepe." It's no wonder he might become mournful. If no one beats his qualifying

Unser (front right), Mosley, and Foyt are almost into turn one, but
the last three rows haven't even crossed the starting line.

time, he will be a starter in the Indy 500. But if someone finds that extra mile per hour, he'll be out of the race, and an entire year's work will go for nothing.

Why do so many drivers risk their lives to run at Indy? After all, there are other 500-mile races at more modern tracks around the country. The answer isn't simple.

For some the prize money draws them back each year. It's a point of pride for the Speedway that the over-$1,600,000 in prize money is the largest in motor racing. The winner will bring home almost $300,000.

Of course, the driver doesn't keep all of the money. The normal split is 50 percent of the purse to the car owner, 40 percent to the driver, and 10 percent to the chief mechanic. But the winner is likely to earn $1,000,000 the following year for doing TV commercials, magazine ads, and as a speaker. And he doesn't share this with anyone.

Every driver who makes the starting field earns something. In 1982 Kevin Cogan caused a crash that wrecked his and three other cars at the start of the race. Still, Cogan and the others each received over $40,000 without even running a lap.

The potential earnings at Indy are so great that drivers have been known to invest their own money in a car just to get to drive in the race. This is called "buying a ride." And for a few it pays off. Frank Lockhart mortgaged his home to drive in the 1926 500—and managed to be in the lead when rain forced a stop to the race.

Together with the money, there's a great deal of publicity for everyone who makes the starting field. Over 4,400 reporters and photographers cover the practice session, qualifying runs, and the race. An estimated 36,000,000 people see the race on TV and another 200,000,000 around the world listen to it over radio. Not much happens at Indy that isn't seen or heard by many millions of people.

Janet Guthrie and car owner Rolla Vollstedt. Guthrie placed twenty-
ninth in 1977, but came back the next year to finish a strong ninth.

This means recognition for a driver who does well. In 1981
rookie Kevin Cogan took a car that had no major sponsors and
finished fourth. He was immediately hired to drive for the famous
Penske Racing Team. And not many people had heard of Janet
Guthrie before 1976, even though she'd been in over 120 road
races. When she became the first woman to qualify for the field in
1977, her feat was reported worldwide.

```
OFFICIAL PRIZE LIST, TIMES AND AVERAGES FOR THE 1982 "500" MILE RACE

FINAL      CAR
POS.       No.    DRIVER                CAR NAME
```

FINAL POS.	CAR No.	DRIVER	CAR NAME
1	20	Gordon Johncock	STP Oil Treatment Special
2	1	Rick Mears	The Gould Charge Penske
3	3	Pancho Carter	Alex Foods Special
4	7	Tom Sneva	Texaco Star
5	10	Al Unser	Longhorn Racing, Inc.
6	91	Don Whittington	The Simoniz Finish
7	42	Jim Hickman	Stroh's March
8	5	Johnny Rutherford	Pennzoil Chaparral
9	28	Herm Johnson	Menard Cashway Lumber Special
10	30	Howdy Holmes	Domino's Pizza/Team Shierson
11	19	Bobby Rahal	Red Roof Inn's March
12	8	Gary Bettenhausen	Kraco Special
13	52	**Hector Rebaque	Carta Blanca
14	53	Danny Sullivan	Forsythe-Brown Racing
15	12	Chip Ganassi	First Commercial Corp. Special
16	94	**Bill Whittington	Whittington Warner Hodgdon
17	68	Michael Chandler	Freeman/Gurney Eagle
18	27	Tom Bigelow	H.B.K. Racing/Vollstedt Eagle
19	14	A.J. Foyt, Jr.	Valvoline-Gilmore
20	34	Johnny Parsons	Silhouette/Tombstone Pizza/WIFE
21	35	George Snider	Cobre Tire
22	25	Danny Ongais	Interscope Racing
23	69	Jerry Sneva	The Great American Spirit
24	39	Chet Fillip	Circle Bar Truck Corral
25	66	Pete Halsmer	Colonial/Pay Less/WISH/Arciero
26	16	Tony Bettenhausen	Provimi Veal
27	75	Dennis Firestone	B.C.V. Racing
28	21	Geoff Brabham	Pentax Super
29	55	Josele Garza	Schlitz Gusto
30	4	Kevin Cogan	Norton Spirit Penske
31	40	Mario Andretti	STP Oil Treatment Special
32	31	Roger Mears	Machinists Union Racing team
33	95	Dale Whittington	Whittington Warner Hodgdon

Miscellaneous Cash Awards

```
X - Cars running at finish          * - Includes lap prize money
# - New all-time record                 and cash accessory awards
                               ** - Penalized two laps -
                                    yellow passing violation
```

The official prize-money list for the 1982 race.

TIME	LAPS	MPH	SPEEDWAY PRIZES	TOTAL PRIZES
3:05:09.14	200X	162.029	$ 187,575.76	$ 290,609.10
3:05:09.30	200X	162.026	107,075.75	215,859.09
3:05:50.96	199X	160.614	72,575.75	103,559.09
3:05:55.17	197	160.668	54,575.75	88,309.09
3:05:42.78	197X	159.116	52,175.75	60,352.75
3:06:02.38	196X	158.031	50,375.75	57,159.09
3:05:42.25	189X	152.662	49,725.75	59,209.09
3:01:03.85	187	154.917	47,195.75	50,329.09
3:05:26.92	186X	150.446	45,845.75	53,454.09
3:05:32.63	186X	150.369	45,095.76	48,679.10
2:51:00.78	174	152.620	44,405.76	47,989.10
2:44:43.33	158	143.879	46,245.76	49,679.09
2:41:10.39	150	139.601	43,115.76	55,115.76
2:23:11.57	148	155.036	42,455.76	46,889.09
2:36:20.66	147	141.035	41,885.76	45,819.09
1:59:58.01	121	151.292	41,345.76	43,779.09
1:45:23.08	104	148.029	43,335.76	48,269.09
2:24:09.81	96	99.887	41,855.76	44,289.09
1:32:26.54	95	154.150	43,905.76	71,239.09
2:08:12.03	92	107.644	39,485.76	42,919.09
1:23:29.98	87	156.288	39,095.76	41,529.09
54:18.19	62	171.261	38,735.76	41,319.09
54:22.42	61	168.280	38,405.76	40,839.09
1:06:44.75	60	134.840	38,105.76	40,539.09
44:14.98	38	128.815	38,835.76	41,269.09
31:13.96	37	177.699	37,595.76	40,429.09
52:37.90	37	105.450	38,885.76	41,319.09
9:51.12	12	182.704	39,705.76	42,139.09
1:00.75	1	148.148	37,055.76	40,489.09
00	0	000	42,435.76	44,769.09
00	0	000	38,845.76	44,279.09
00	0	000	36,785.76	41,719.09
00	0	000	38,255.76	40,355.76
				3,000.00
				$2,067,475.00#*
			$1,643,000.00#	

Mario Andretti doing a pre-race radio interview.

But many drivers who return year after year to Indy are already rich and famous. Mario Andretti is a World Champion Formula One race car driver. Johnny Rutherford, Bobby Unser, and Al Unser have each won Indy three times already. And A. J. Foyt has been coming to the Brickyard for over twenty-six years, breaking just about every record along the way.

For these and other veteran drivers, it is their competitive streak that makes them return to Indy. They know that only the very best drivers and machines will make the starting field and finish the race.

"I'm not drawn back every year by a lot of money," A. J. Foyt said. "I come back because of the competition and because I enjoy it."

Another driver may have said it best: "Sure, there are other races. But there's only one Indy."

A fire fighter and race official watch as Johnny Rutherford's Pennzoil Chaparral gets fuel. The entire stop took nine seconds.

3

Getting It All Together

Johnny Rutherford pulls his Pennzoil Chaparral down low in turn four and glides into pit lane. At the beginning of pit lane, Rutherford goes over a rough section of the track. At over 100 mph the car bounces wildly for a second or two.

To his right, blurs of red, yellow, and blue streak past. These are the other race cars blasting down the front straightaway. To his left, the pits are crammed with hundreds of people—pit men, race officials, fire fighters, photographers, and TV crews. Thousands more loom above him in the grandstands.

Rutherford watches two race cars roar down pit lane to rejoin the race. Then he spots his car's color and number on a sign at the end of a long pole. Rutherford pulls into his pit and brakes sharply, the nose of the car even with the sign.

Even before the car is fully stopped, his five pitmen have vaulted the cement wall. In less than a second, the crew swarms around the car, each man going to his assigned spot to do his job. For the next fifteen to twenty seconds, Johnny Rutherford is no longer in control of his car.

When a car is on the track, everyone's attention is glued to it and the driver. They are all that racing fans are aware of. But behind the scenes, hundreds of highly skilled people are required to put the car together and keep it running smoothly.

Years ago it was possible for a few individuals to put together a car and run at Indy. That's how Andy Granatelli got started in 1946. Granatelli bought a dusty race car that had been sitting in a

With the care and precision of a team of surgeons, the Penske mechanics put together a new Indy car.

garage for eleven years! Then he and some friends cleaned up the car, tinkered with the engine and hauled it to the Speedway. Granatelli broke the one-lap speed record while qualifying and managed to finish twenty-first in the race—an impressive showing for a rookie in an ancient car.

Today it's just about impossible to take an old car and hope to qualify for the race. The constant change in body shape and engines makes even a two- or three-year-old car out of date. And the cars go so fast that the slightest imperfection can cause it to go out of control and crash.

These days a car engineer and Fiberglas designer will work together to create an exterior body with the least wind resistance. A wing man will design and build the two wings that hold the car on the track. Someone else handles the brake systems.

Even the tires have to be made specifically for the Speedway. Each year Goodyear Tire and Rubber Company has about 200 people involved in the design, testing, and manufacture of the Eagle Speedway Special racing tires.

Another strip of rubber is added. The drum will then be compressed and heated to form the tire.

On a cold March day, Rutherford tests the new tires while Goodyear technicians watch. The tent shields the engine from winds that might cool it down too much.

Goodyear works closely with the race teams to be sure their tires are compatible with the changing car designs. It puts together many different rubber compounds searching for the tires that grip and wear well. Then in March, Goodyear takes the tires to the Speedway to actually test them at speed.

Goodyear picks the best tires from the test and makes around 1,500 of them. These are given to all race teams for free. In return, every car carries several Goodyear stickers.

The modern Indy car is so complex that even the most skilled automotive builders will use racing parts made by other companies. In 1981 the Machinists Union decided to enter Indy car racing. But instead of trying to design and build a car themselves,

Machinists Union Racing Team

Penske PC-9B Specifications

CONSTRUCTOR:	Penske Cars
CHASSIS:	Aluminum Monocoque with Fabricated Steel Bulkheads
BODYWORK:	Fiberglass Mouldings by Marchant and Cox, Ltd.
PAINT FINISHES:	Ditzler Automotive Finishes, PPG Industries, Inc.
SUSPENSION:	Inboard Springs and Dampers Front and Rear, Operated by Top Rocker Arm; Front and Rear Lower "A" Arms of Streamlined Tubing
STEERING:	Penske Rack and Pinion
BRAKES:	Lockheed
SHOCK ABSORBERS:	Monroe
HOSE AND FITTINGS:	Aeroquip
WHEELS:	Penske
TIRES:	Goodyear Eagle Speedway Special
CLUTCH:	Borg & Beck
GEARBOX:	Hewland LG 500 4-speed
ENGINE:	Turbocharged Cosworth Ford DFX
	8 Cylinder - Twin Overhead Camshafts
	2.6 Litres - 159 CID
HORSEPOWER:	700 @ 10,000 RPM with 48 Inches of Boost
ENGINE PREPARATION:	Penske Racing, Inc.
ENGINE BEARINGS:	Gould Clevite 77
TURBOCHARGER:	Schwitzer
SPARKPLUGS:	Champion
IGNITION:	Mallory
STARTING POWER:	Sears Diehard Battery
FUEL:	Methanol, Valvoline Oil Company, Division of Ashland Oil
FUEL CAPACITY:	40 Gallons
FUEL SYSTEM:	Cosworth Fuel Injection
FUEL CELL:	Goodyear Crashworthy
LUBRICANTS:	Valvoline
OIL FILTER:	STP
WHEEL BASE:	108"
FRONT TRACK:	65"
REAR TRACK:	62"
CHASSIS WIDTH	62"
CHASSIS HEIGHT:	32"
OVERALL LENGTH:	15'
WEIGHT:	1,500 lbs.
WEIGHT DISTRIBUTION:	37/63

This specifications sheet for the Machinists Union car shows the
source of the various racing parts.

The manager of the Penske Racing Team, Derrick Walker, discusses rule changes with an official.

they had one made by the Penske Racing Team. And even Penske couldn't do the job without the help of seventeen other companies. One was even needed to do the paint job.

Once a car is together, the racing team takes over. Each team is headed by a crew chief or team manager. The crew chief is like the coach of a football team. He coordinates the work of the mechanics and their assistants. He'll drill the pit crew and other team members. And the crew chief is the one who is in contact with the driver during the race.

Each team also has a chief mechanic. The chief mechanic is

responsible for all of the work on the car. He'll make sure the team has enough parts and will decide what jobs everyone will do on the car.

On smaller teams the chief mechanic might also be the crew chief, as well as one of the pit crew. Larger teams will have a separate crew chief, chief mechanic, and team for every car they bring to the track.

In addition to these people, a number of others are needed on the racing team to keep the car running smoothly. For instance, during the race, two people are stationed in the pit to check the

While one scorer takes a break, the other notes car speed and laps completed.

car's speed and count the number of laps it does. These are the scorers. A race car is allowed to carry only 40 gallons of fuel and gets about 1½ miles to the gallon. This means the car has to be refueled about every twenty-five laps. If the scorers make a mistake, the driver can find himself rolling down the back straightaway without a drop of fuel.

Scorers also keep track of where the other cars in the field are, their speeds and the number of pit stops they take. This information lets their driver know exactly how he's doing in the race and helps him decide whether he should speed up or take it easy. Often the driver's wife will be one of the scorers.

Each team also has a boardman. Today every team uses a two-way radio that lets the crew chief talk with the driver while he's on the track. But the noise and vibration of the car can make it hard for the driver to hear what is being said. To avoid confusion, the boardman relays messages to the driver.

The boardman is positioned inside the concrete wall of the front straightaway directly across from his car's pit. He receives his information from the crew chief over a two-way radio set. Then he scribbles it onto a chalkboard and holds it up so the passing driver can see it. The other side of the board might have the word IN printed on it in large letters. This lets the driver know he has to pit the next time around.

Sometimes the scribbled messages seem pretty strange because they're written in shorthand. For example, "P3" tells the driver that he has to pit for fuel in three laps; "L57" means he's gone fifty-seven laps. To let the driver know he's leading by five seconds, the sign will say "+5," while "−8" indicates he's eight seconds behind the leader. The boardman also relays the car's speed with a simple "189."

The best-known part of any race team, aside from the driver, is the five-man pit crew. Each man has a specific job to perform when the car comes in. Before race day, members of the pit crew

The boardman for Rick Mears tells him to come "IN." Behind him, Tom Sneva's team does a fast tire change and refueling. The man in front of Sneva's car will let him know when he can pull out of the pit safely.

practice scrambling over the wall and getting into position with the fuel hose, vent hose, air wrenches, and tires. They'll practice this for days until they can do it quickly and flawlessly. The pit crew knows that every second wasted during a stop means hundreds of feet lost on the track.

47

The Machinists Union pit crew dashes into position. During practice drills such as this the car's engine is always off to avoid any chance of fire.

The ritual of the pit stop is just about the same every time.

The refueler attaches the fuel hose at the left side of the car. Another man puts the vent hose in on the top just behind the driver. The vent hose releases air from the fuel cell so the fuel flows in easily. Fuel is added to the car every time it comes in.

Meanwhile, the air-jack man dashes around to the right side of the car and inserts the air hose. Compressed air pushes down four metal bars that are located near each wheel. These raise the car up off the ground a few inches. Each tire is checked quickly for wear or cuts by the two wheel men.

They may look like spacemen, but it's only Don Whittington's pit crew wearing fire-resistant head stockings.

While fuel is added, Whittington gets right side tires. If the fireman seems nervous that's because he's standing next to the 240-gallon tank of methanol fuel.

Pit stop over, Whittington gets a helpful shove from his pitmen.

Usually, the right side tires have to be changed three times during the race. The constant left turns cause these tires to wear down faster. The left side tires might have to be changed once, although they can stay on for the entire race if the car is handling well.

If the pit crew does its job smoothly, the driver can duck into the pits and have all the work done in a matter of seconds. In 1981 Bobby Unser pitted ten times on his way to victory. His longest stop was only eighteen seconds!

But it's important that the work be done with care, as well as with speed. A wheel nut that is put on incorrectly can work its way off very quickly.

There are two other important parts to every racing team, although hardly anyone ever thinks of them. One is the owner. The other is the car's sponsors.

Wally Dallenbach had to be surprised and angry when his right rear tire popped off. The car body rubbing along the track makes sparks.

Car owner Roger Penske with Rick Mears.

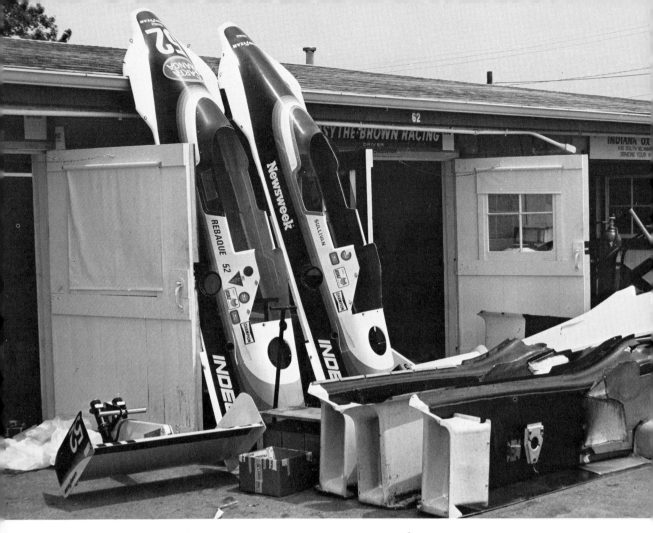

Just some of the spare parts a team must have.

The owners are usually extremely rich businessmen. A few, like Roger Penske, Dan Gurney, and Andy Granatelli, were once race car drivers who now own companies that make automotive parts. But most owners run companies that have nothing to do with cars or car parts. They simply love Indy car racing. Owner Jim

Gilmore is so enthusiastic he has one of A. J. Foyt's Coyote Indy cars parked in his den.

An owner puts up almost all of the money needed to build the car, and to pay the driver, mechanics, and other team members. He also pays for feeding and housing the entire team during the month of May. All of this costs a great deal of money. A Cosworth engine costs about $45,000, and a chassis goes for $40,000. Costs go up because most teams come to the Speedway with three engines and three chassis, plus enough spare parts to build an entire car.

A small race team costs about $250,000: $150,000 to have the

Kevin Cogan of the Penske Racing Team. The major sponsor for his car gets its name in larger letters.

Gordon Johncock, two-time Indy 500 winner, in his racing suit covered with sponsors' patches.

car built and $100,000 for parts and other expenses. The giant Penske team costs around $2,300,000 a year.

The sponsors will put up money for their teams. They'll also supply parts. This can be a big help if you consider that a·fuel cell for an Indy car costs $4,500.

Sponsors, unlike owners, don't share in any of the prize money. For their contribution, each sponsor gets to put his company's name on the car. And the driver will wear the sponsors' patches on his driving suit or be part of an advertising campaign. In a way, the car and driver become 200-mph billboards for everything from automotive parts to beer to designer jeans. The sponsors hope that race fans will see and remember the names of their products.

Getting a good Indy car on the track takes a lot of people and a lot of money. Many hope to earn some money from the race. Others participate because they love motor racing. But once the car is on the track these people tend to fade into the background.

"It's hard sometimes," one chief mechanic said. "You work and work, and you don't get credit. The driver is god and you're in the background. But let's face it," he adds. "The driver's the one who sticks his neck out. He's the one who gets in there and runs at 200 miles per hour."

Ultimately, it always boils down to the driver and his car. Each is tested to the point of breaking, by the speed and the difficult track. And sometimes, no matter how hard everyone on the team has worked, something can go seriously wrong.

Phil Krueger, a second after hitting the wall.

4

Losing to the Odds

Phil Krueger had completed two good qualifying laps in his number 89 Eagle. He cruised through turns one and two of his third lap and charged down the long back straightaway. When he entered turn three he was doing 186 mph.

Suddenly Krueger got the car's nose too low in the turn. He sensed his speed slowing and corrected hard to the right. Too hard. Car 89 went into a 240-foot-long skid and smashed into the wall. The thudding crash ripped up the entire right side of the car. The Fiberglas and aluminum bodywork peeled back as if a giant can opener had been used on it. The rear wing loosened and tilted at an odd angle.

The car continued to slide along the wall for 80 feet. The concrete ripped off the right rear tire and bits of the car's body flew into the air. An oil line ruptured and a jagged tail of fire appeared.

The car slipped away from the wall still traveling at well over 100 mph. The rushing air pulled at the bodywork until the right side fell off. The front wing flew into the air too. The car finally came to a stop 1,200 feet later in the infield of turn four.

Phil Krueger had challenged the dangerous Speedway and lost. His car was completely destroyed. But miraculously, Phil Krueger survived.

The crash of an Indy car is always a spectacular sight. Bits of Fiberglas and aluminum fly all over the place. Tires tear loose and bounce down the track. But as terrible as they might appear at first, most crashes at Indy are surprisingly safe. Krueger suf-

The right rear wheel is ripped off and oil catches fire.

The flying debris is kept from sailing into the grandstands by the 20-foot-tall safety fence.

At this point Krueger's slide is only half over. The front wing is in the air near the car.

fered a few broken ribs, a fractured shoulder, and facial burns. These are relatively minor when you consider that he hit a concrete wall at over 180 mph and his crash covered a quarter-mile of the track. Krueger was released from the hospital after three days and was back driving several months later. He's okay today because of the unique design of his car.

In the past, designers felt that the stronger they built the entire car, the safer the driver would be. The car's body was made of heavy sheet metal. The frame was of rigid steel. Mauri Rose was driving a car like this in 1946 when he lost control and rammed the wall. Only a few bits of metal and his left front tire came off.

Oddly enough, the problem with these cars was that they held together too well in a crash. With the tires still on, a car could climb the wall or begin to bounce down the track. The narrow shape let it roll over and over. Sometimes a car bounced so much it would begin to somersault from its nose to tail for hundreds of feet down the track. The force of the initial crash would often ram the steering wheel into the driver's chest. He was injured even more by being tossed around inside his car.

But the Fiberglas body and light metal parts of a modern Indy

Mauri Rose's car climbed the concrete wall on impact, but only a few pieces of metal and tire came off.

All that was left of Krueger's car.

car are actually designed to fall apart on impact. As the car falls apart, it has less chance to bounce. And because the car is over 6 feet wide, it usually doesn't roll over. Instead, the car drops to the pavement and slides along harmlessly on its belly.

To further protect the driver, the cockpit is surrounded by reinforced aluminum. So while the remains of Phil Krueger's car look gruesome, the most important part—where he was sitting— is still intact.

An Indy car has a number of other safety features built into it. A roll bar behind the driver protects his head in case the car does flip over. An on-board fire extinguisher can be activated by the driver if a fire breaks out. And the steering wheel is padded and made to collapse on impact.

To reduce the chance of being tossed around inside the car, the cockpit is built very narrow. And the padded seat wraps around the sides of the driver. The driver has to actually squeeze himself into the tiny compartment. Then a wide shoulder harness and seat belt secure him in place.

A crew member buckles Foyt into his car.

There isn't much room inside the cockpit. Just enough so the driver's hands can steer and shift gears, while his feet work the clutch, accelerator, and brake. It's such a tight fit that a crew member has to buckle the driver's shoulder harness and seat belt.

The close-up of Vern Schuppan on page 64 shows other safety items. The most obvious is his crash helmet. The helmet is well padded and has a shatterproof plastic visor. A shoulder strap prevents the helmet from popping off during a crash. Schuppan is also wearing a neck brace. This limits the movement of his head and reduces neck injuries.

Even his clothes are made for safety. His socks and shoes, underwear, head stocking, gloves, and driving suit are all made of a fire-resistant cloth called Nomex. If a fire breaks out in the car, the driver's Nomex clothes will give him 30 seconds of protection. The only part of his body not covered by Nomex are his eyes.

All of these safety features combine to make driving—and crashing—at Indy safer than it has ever been. During the first sixty-four years of Indy, sixty-one people were killed. In the last ten years only one, Gordon Smiley, has been killed. So while most high-speed crashes leave the $150,000 car torn apart, the majority of drivers walk away uninjured. Still, there are some types of accidents that can be very dangerous even in an Indy car.

One can occur when the car goes airborne. This can happen if the front tire of one car hits another car's tire. The tire will actually climb up and over the other tire. The front of the car will leave the ground, changing the angle of the front and rear wings. At this point, the car loses its ground effects. The air that is supposed to push the wings and car down against the track will lift it up instead. The light cars have been known to "fly" over 300 feet before crashing. The force of the impact can break apart the reinforced cockpit.

Fortunately, the quick reactions of a driver can reduce the

Everything is expensive in motor racing. A complete racing suit plus
helmet costs $1,200. Most drivers bring two suits.

chance of losing the ground effects. If he sees he's going to hit another car, the driver will lock up the brakes. This forces the nose of the car to dip low and usually stops the car from bouncing. And since the tires aren't turning, they can't push the car higher into the air.

Car 38 hit the wall while qualifying and went airborne. A Speedway photographer thinks twice about taking a shot of the accident.

The worst crashes involve head-on collisions with the wall. The impact from this kind of crash can completely disintegrate a car.

A driver heading into the wall will lock up his brakes to slow the car. Then as the car goes into a slide, the driver will maneuver it so the tires and side take most of the impact. If the driver is lucky, he can minimize the damage to the car and to himself.

But the thing that worries drivers most isn't hitting another car or the wall. It's fire. Indy cars don't use gasoline. They run on an alcohol-based fuel called methanol, because it burns cleaner in the engine.

Methanol is highly flammable. And it burns without any flames or smoke. The only sign that a methanol fire is burning is intense heat shimmers. Because of this, fire fighters, pitmen, and even the driver may not know a fire is burning until the car is completely engulfed.

During the 1981 500, fuel was spewed over car number 6, its driver, Rick Mears, and his refueling man. The second the fuel hit the hot exhaust pipe the car and the two men were ablaze.

The refueler began dancing around the pit trying to beat out the invisible flames and get someone's attention. No one noticed he was on fire, so the refueler ran to a nighboring pit where an alert fire fighter blasted him with his carbon dioxide fire extinguisher.

Meanwhile, Mears released his harness and leaped from his car. He stumbled against the pit wall and a crew member from another team tossed a bucket of water over him. By this time, fifteen or so fire fighters had gathered around the burning car. A white haze of carbon dioxide filled the pit area as they put out the fire on Mears and his car.

The thirty-five-second fire completely destroyed the car. Mears and his refueler received third-degree burns and had to be hospitalized.

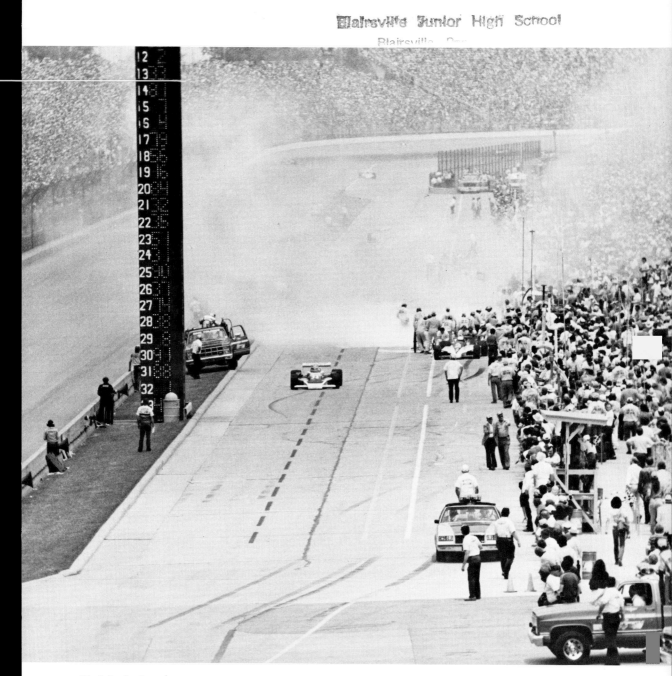

Behind the carbon dioxide haze, Mears, his refueler, and his car are
on fire. But the race goes on as other cars charge into the pits.

After Mear's fire, extra firemen were stationed in the pits. Here a safety crew and firemen spray Hector Rebaque's car just seconds after it caught fire.

The fire fighters and safety crews are the drivers' final line of protection at the track. There are over 250 fire fighters at the race; 3 are assigned to each pit, while another 51 can move to anywhere in the pits where trouble develops. There are also twenty safety trucks positioned at various locations around the track.

At the start of the 1982 race Kevin Cogan lost control of his car, tapped A. J. Foyt's wheels and skidded. Cogan was broadsided by Andretti and spun around some more. A second later car 91 clipped Cogan's machine and sheared off the front right tire. But even before the tire hit the ground the safety truck was rolling toward the scene of the accident.

A safety crew can be at the scene of a crash in a few seconds. Their first job is to put out any fire and see if the driver is injured. If the driver is trapped in the crumpled wreck, a spreader can pry apart the metal. The spreader is called the "jaws of life."

As the crew begins working to remove the driver, one of the track's nineteen ambulances will arrive. Once freed, the driver is taken to the track hospital.

The hospital has a staff of 285 doctors, nurses, and inhalation specialists. This might sound like a lot of medical personnel, but remember that 400,000 people come to watch the race. And of these, over 500 will have injuries that require medical attention.

Most of the time the doctors can care for a driver if his injuries are not too serious. But if he is hurt badly, two helicopters are ready to fly the driver to a nearby hospital. A driver who has to stay in the hospital is said to be doing "sheet time."

The cars haven't even stopped spinning and the safety crew is rolling.

A run-in with the wall ripped off the right side of this car. It was carried to its garage for repairs.

While the driver is being cared for, the safety crew has to get the damaged car off the track. If it can still roll on its wheels the car will be pushed off the track to the garages. If it can't roll it will be lifted and hauled away. Then the safety crew cleans up the track of small bits of metal that can puncture a tire or oil that might cause another car to spin out.

There's no escaping the fact that Indy is a tough and dangerous track to drive on. Of the 105 cars entered in 1981, 21 of them were involved in some sort of accident. And as the speeds go up so do the chances that something will go wrong.

The amazing thing is that serious injuries have been reduced. Part of this is due to the drivers' high degree of skill. But it's also a tribute to the improved design of the cars and the army of fire fighters, safety crews, and medical personnel.

The final pace lap of the 1982 race. The large building on the right is the master control tower. Officials keep track of the race from here. The tall, narrow scoring pylon lets the spectators know the position of every car. The small structure at left halfway up the straightaway is where the flagger stands.

5

From Start to Finish

It all begins with the ritual command: "Gentlemen, start your engines." Instantly, thirty-three racing engines jump to life with a high-pitched roar.

One minute later, two pace cars begin moving slowly around the 2½-mile track. Behind them, in eleven rows of three, the race cars follow, weaving back and forth sharply to warm their engines and tires. After two laps, one pace car pulls off the road. The other increases its speed to over 100 mph.

Now pace car and racers circle the track for a third time, each race car maintaining its position in the starting formation. Mears has the pole, with Cogan and Foyt next to him. Behind them, a few drivers check out their two-way radios to make sure they have contact with their pits. Others look at the gauges to see if everything is working perfectly. They have forgotten the months of sweat and the thousands of dollars that have gone into the preparation of their cars. They've blocked out everything that might take their attention away from driving.

As they come through turn four, the pace car pulls into the pit area and Mears increases his speed to around 140 mph. The other cars charge to keep up with Mears. They're not allowed to pass Mears, but they don't want to give him a running start either. The starter checks their positioning as they come out of the turn and head down the straightaway.

The drivers glance at the starter, hoping to see the green flag that will send the race off. They might not be thinking it at the moment, but the drivers know that the most dangerous part of the race is the start. Indy is the only major motor race where the cars line up in rows of three. With the track so narrow and the cars bunched up like this, an out-of-control car can do nothing except bounce off the wall and into other cars. That's what happened in 1966 when fourteen cars were involved in a fiery crash at the start.

Finally, the starter drops the green flag. The cars blast ahead, accelerating through the first two turns. Mears and the rest of the lead cars cause so much air disturbance that cars in the middle of the pack can be sucked along, as if they were caught in a tornado.

A moment after this photo was taken in 1966, the cars involved in the crash were engulfed by flames. At that time the fence around the track was quite low so tires and debris flew into the stands.

A formation of cars sweeps through turn one. Gordon Johncock is in the middle (ahead of car 3).

Off turn two, Gordon Johncock wastes no time in charging past five cars to move up with the leaders. Halfway down the back straightaway, he's even with Rutherford and doing 180 mph.

For the first five or ten laps the cars that qualified up front will run just about full out. The drivers are trying to establish position in the race and to see how their cars perform against the others. Most important, they want to pull away from the slower traffic.

The cars at the back go out fast too, although they have little chance of staying close to the leaders. The few fast cars in the back will charge past the slower ones, using the opening laps to gain on the front-runners. They don't want the leaders to get too far away from them. Mario Andretti started the 1981 race in thirty-second position. Andretti picked his way through traffic relentlessly until he was in tenth position after only fourteen laps!

Once they finish the initial laps, the drivers will ease into a slightly slower racing speed. It would be impossible to run a car full out for the entire 500 miles. The car would eat up too much fuel. And the heat and stress would probably cause the engine to blow.

Instead, drivers settle into their cars and begin to run their race plans. Al Unser uses this opportunity to take the lead, hoping to keep the pace just fast enough to get well away from the field. Rutherford, Johncock, and Foyt tuck themselves in behind Unser.

Others, like Mears, prefer to go just fast enough to stay close to the leaders.

"What's the use of running ahead of everybody all day if you can't even finish?" asks Mears. "I spend half or three-fourths of the race trying to finish and the last fourth trying to move to the front."

The slower drivers will drive much the same kind of race as Mears does. They know that if they hope to ever drive for one of the big teams, they have to prove they can finish strong even with

Slower cars dueling down the back straight.

a slower car. Besides, the higher they manage to finish, the bigger their paychecks will be.

As the race progresses, all of the little things the drivers have learned about the track during the practice session come into play.

They know they should stay two feet from the wall in turn two because there's a slight hump in the road surface there. They know where the wind can make cornering tricky. Most of all, they're trying to keep their cars in the groove through the turns and drive a smooth race.

Even though Mears has settled into his car, he can't let his mind wander. He's got to be ready for each turn. And he has to check his rearview mirror to see if anyone has pulled up on him.

Three cars follow the groove through a turn.

On race day, this will be the driver's home for three and a half hours.

Like stock cars, Indy cars can "draft." The lead car cuts through the air and pushes it aside. The following car doesn't have to work to plow through the air. This driver can ease up on the accelerator, save fuel, and still go as fast as the car ahead of him. And if he steps on the gas to pass, the draft will slingshot him past the lead car.

Stock cars can draft for many laps in a row because their engines are water-cooled by large radiators. But an Indy car only has two small radiators inside the side vents. So if a car stays in the draft of another for more than twenty-five seconds, the radiators won't get enough air. This will overheat the engine and probably cause it to blow. To avoid overheating, drivers will slide out of the draft often to keep the engine at proper running tem-

A spinning car just in front forced the driver of car 53 to lock up his wheels.

perature. Then they'll move back into the draft to save a few more seconds of fuel.

Each time the driver shoots down the front straight he'll glance at his boardman. Danny Ongais sees that he's seven seconds (about a half-mile) behind the leader and increases his speed slightly. He started the race in the sixth row, but has been able to move up only a few positions.

Down the back straight he checks his five gauges. They tell him the temperature of the oil and engine exhaust, oil and turbocharger pressure, and the number of engine revolutions he's turning per minute. Ongais can't take time to study each gauge and note the specific numbers. To make the check easy, the gauges are positioned so their needles point straight up if everything is okay.

Just as Ongais looks up from his gauges, he sees an eruption of smoke and flame about 800 feet in front of him. The suspension system on Josele Garza's car has broken, sending him into the wall and ripping up the right side. As the car drifts to the middle of the track, the rear tire comes loose and begins rolling toward the infield.

Ongais has about two seconds to decide what he'll do before he rams the crippled car. If possible, he doesn't want to lock up the wheels to stop. Doing this will wear a flat spot on the tires and ruin the car's handling.

Instead, he pulls his car up high, close to the wall. Garza's car is still rolling toward the infield and this is the clearest path. As he plows through the hazy smoke left behind by the accident, he feels a sharp thump on the right side. He's hit a chunk of Garza's car. Before he reaches the next turn, his steering becomes difficult as the front tire goes flat. He drops low on the track, knowing he'll have to coast into the pits for a tire change and to see if any other damage was done. Vern Schuppan, Bill Whittington, and a string of other cars pass him easily. Ongais knows he'll be down two laps before he can get his car back on the track again.

An accident always brings out the flagger's yellow caution flag. A pace car will pull out onto the track and all the cars line up in single file behind it according to their position in the race. They will circle the track at 80 mph while the safety crew helps the driver and clears off the wreck.

No one is allowed to pass during a yellow. But a car can pull into the pits for fuel and tires if it wants. When it exits the pits, it has to blend into the pack or simply fall in at the end of the line.

While the yellow flag is out, the cars will snake around the track. Each time they approach the start/finish line, the drivers have their eyes on the flagger. The flagger controls the race from his perch above the track.

A yellow will keep them going around the track. But if the accident is very bad, the flagger can halt the race with a red flag.

As the race wears on, the cars bunch up according to speed.

In addition to slowing or stopping the race, the flagger can order any car off the track with a black flag. He might do this if he sees the car engine smoking.

The flagger can also tell drivers to move over so faster cars can pass them by waving a blue-and-yellow checkered flag. A white flag indicates there is only one lap left in the race; a black-and-white checkered flag signals the end of the race.

Each time the drivers come down the front straightaway during the caution, they'll look for the green flag. When it drops, the cars go roaring off again.

All during the race, drivers will battle for position, each trying to improve his standing. On pages 84–85, Bobby Unser (3) tries to pass Andretti on the front straight. But Andretti has enough power to pull up and even with Unser as they approach turn one.

If Unser had maintained his half-car lead, Andretti would have had to slow to let Unser in front of him. This is called "giving the driver the road." Since they were even, Unser had to make a quick decision. He could have raced Andretti through the turn without cutting in front of him. But if he got up a little too high, he'd find himself in the marbles. Or he could back off and wait for another chance to pass. Unser backed off this time.

With each lap turned, the drivers, cars, and crews are tested. A minor part on Rutherford's car breaks and he has to pull into the pits, hoping the problem can be repaired before he loses too many laps. Johnny Parsons's neck begins to stiffen after making 400 left turns. But the drivers continue to coax their cars and themselves through more laps, always watching for any change in their cars.

Foyt checks his gauges and sees that the number of engine revolutions goes down when he's in the turn. This is a sign that he's losing speed in the turns, usually because the wings are pushing down too hard against the track. He's forced to pit to have the angle of the wings adjusted. When he rejoins the race, he's three laps down.

A classic 190-mph confrontation down the front straight. The fans of
Andretti (40) cheer as he goes into turn one ahead of Unser. Later,
Unser overtook Andretti.

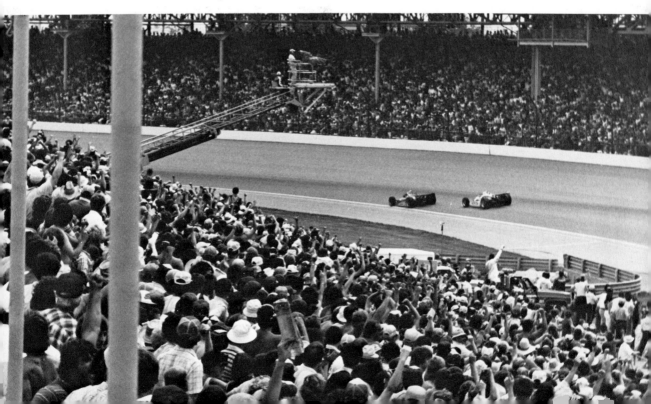

As the cars pass the 450-mile mark, their teams begin preparing for the final laps. The speeds will increase as each driver "dials up his boost." This forces more fuel through the turbocharger and increases horsepower and speed. Drivers can't dial up for the entire race because they'd eat up too much fuel. They have to carefully consider when they want this extra power.

The most important event in the race's closing stages is the last pit stop. This is usually for fuel only, although a driver might want new tires to run full out on. Rick Mears comes in for fuel with just ten laps remaining. But in his eagerness, Mears nearly hits the rear of a slow-moving car and has to brake sharply. No damage is done to his tires, but Mears has lost valuable time following the slower-moving car down pit lane. A lap later, Gordon Johncock comes blasting into the pits, weaving around slower-moving cars. Johncock takes on a dash of fuel, then leaves.

On the track again, Johncock's fast pitting puts him just in front of Mears. Al Unser has dropped back to third, ten seconds off the pace. For the final twenty miles, Mears and Johncock duel each other for the lead at over 190 mph.

Down every straightaway Mears attempts to pass, but he never quite has the speed. Johncock takes the checkered flag with only 16/100 of a second separating his car from Mears's. It is the closest finish in Indy history, and Johncock may owe the win as much to his quick pitting as to his driving skill.

Each year, moments after the race is over, the winner is swarmed by people as he receives the famous Borg-Warner trophy. Race officials try to decide each driver's final position—and the prize money his team will receive.

Meanwhile, the cars still on the track at the finish get pushed into the garage area. Tools are packed away. The spare engines, Fiberglas bodies and parts are put into the van for shipping. It's quiet in the garages except for bits of conversation among the teams. Many drivers probably feel they could have won—or at least placed their cars a little higher in the standing—with just a little luck.

Already they're examining where they lost time and wondering how to get a few more miles per hour out of their engines. After all, the next Indy 500 is only a year away.

Johncock edges Mears in the closest Indy finish ever.

Glossary

At speed is the time when any car is running as fast as it can go.

Being loose happens when the rear tires slide out more than the front tires in a turn.

Blowing an engine means pressure inside the engine causes it to explode. This is also referred to as *cooking the engine.*

Brain fade happens when a racer's concentration wanders from his driving.

Buying a ride is when a person invests money in a car in order to drive it.

Drafting occurs when one driver uses the car ahead to push air aside and reduce wind resistance.

Giving the driver the road happens when any driver gets a half-car lead over another. The trailing car must slow up and allow the lead car to get in front.

The groove is the easiest and fastest route through the turns.

Jaws of life refers to a machine used to pry apart metal after a crash in order to free a trapped driver.

Locking up the brakes happens when a driver applies the brakes too hard and causes all four wheels to stop turning instantly. This often results in a skid.

The man on the bubble is the driver with the slowest qualifying time. Since he will be eliminated from the race if anyone can go faster, the man on the bubble often watches the remaining qualifying runs with a very gloomy expression. When this happens, he's said to be *hanging crepe.*

The marbles refers to an area high in the turns where bits of rubber worn from the tires collect.

Push occurs when the front tires slide along the pavement in a turn. If the sliding is very bad, the car is said to be *plowing.*

Sheet time is any time a driver stays in the hospital because of crash-related injuries.

Winners of the Indy 500

1911	Ray Harroun	74.59
1912	Joe Dawson	78.72
1913	Jules Goux	75.933
1914	Rene Thomas	82.47
1915	Ralph DePalma	89.84
1916	Dario Resta (300-mile race)	84.00
1917-18	World War I—No races scheduled	
1919	Howard Wilcox	88.05
1920	Gaston Chevrolet	88.62
1921	Tommy Milton	89.62
1922	Jimmy Murphy	94.48
1923	Tommy Milton	90.95
1924	Joe Boyer	
	L. L. Corum	98.23
1925	Peter DePaolo	101.13
1926	Frank Lockhart (400 miles, rain)	95.904
1927	George Souders	97.545
1928	Louis Meyer	99.482
1929	Ray Keech	97.585
1930	Billy Arnold	100.448
1931	Louis Schneider	96.629
1932	Fred Frame	104.144
1933	Louis Meyer	104.162
1934	Bill Cummings	104.863
1935	Kelly Petillo	106.240
1936	Louis Meyer	109.069
1937	Wilbur Shaw	113.580
1938	Floyd Roberts	117.200
1939	Wilbur Shaw	115.035
1940	Wilbur Shaw	114.277
1941	Mauri Rose	
	Floyd Davis	115.117

1942-45	World War II—No races scheduled	
1946	George Robson	*114.820*
1947	Mauri Rose	*116.338*
1948	Mauri Rose	*119.814*
1949	Bill Holland	*121.327*
1950	Johnnie Parsons (345 miles, rain)	*124.002*
1951	Lee Wallard	*126.244*
1952	Troy Ruttman	*128.922*
1953	Bill Vukovich	*128.740*
1954	Bill Vukovich	*130.840*
1955	Bob Sweikert	*128.209*
1956	Pat Flaherty	*128.490*
1957	Sam Hanks	*135.601*
1958	Jim Bryan	*133.791*
1959	Rodger Ward	*135.857*
1960	Jim Rathmann	*138.767*
1961	A. J. Foyt, Jr.	*139.130*
1962	Rodger Ward	*140.293*
1963	Parnelli Jones	*143.137*
1964	A. J. Foyt, Jr.	*147.350*
1965	Jim Clark	*150.686*
1966	Graham Hill	*144.317*
1967	A. J. Foyt, Jr.	*151.207*
1968	Bobby Unser	*152.882*
1969	Mario Andretti	*156.867*
1970	Al Unser	*155.749*
1971	Al Unser	*157.735*
1972	Mark Donohue	*162.962*
1973	Gordon Johncock (332.5 miles, rain)	*159.036*
1974	Johnny Rutherford	*158.589*
1975	Bobby Unser (435 miles, rain)	*149.213*
1976	Johnny Rutherford (255 miles, rain)	*148.725*
1977	A. J. Foyt, Jr.	*161.331*
1978	Al Unser	*161.363*
1979	Rick Mears	*158.899*
1980	Johnny Rutherford	*142.862*
1981	Bobby Unser	*138.928*
1982	Gordon Johncock	*162.029*
1983	Tom Sneva	*162.117*

Index

Page numbers in *italics* refer to captions.